WHAT'S IN THIS BOOK?

As big as it gets   5

What is happening
The nature of the illness   6
Who is ill?   7
Living in a different way   9

Talking with children
Dealing with the truth   12
Ages and stages   13
Telling the children   14
Balancing hope and honesty   16
What to tell and when   17
Choosing the right words   17
Explaining change   18
Questions children may ask   19

Riding the emotional rollercoaster
Feelings, thoughts and behaviours   22
Reacting to the news   23
Give and take   23
Feeling secure   24
When more help may be needed   26
Looking after yourself   27

Preparing for change
When treatment is necessary   30
Explaining side effects   30
If treatment is not successful   31
Care with words   32
Telling family and friends   33
Visiting the hospital or hospice   34
Staying away from home   35
When recovery is unlikely   36
When death is imminent   37
Preparing for the future   38

Looking ahead
The role of schools   48
School support   49
An altered future   51
Where to seek further support   52

Books and resources   54

A note about language:

We use the term 'children' to include children and young people

When we refer to 'parents' or 'siblings', we include the rich variety of family relationships, including, for example, step-parents and half-siblings

"'We don't want this to be happening. We want the worst thing to affect the children to be not having the right phone or something. They are too young to face the changes that are coming. But they will come, so somehow we have to find the way to keep them feeling safe and involved and loved. And to still be allowed to have fun. Somehow."
Chris and Luisa

AS BIG AS IT GETS

In this book we aim to share the experience and knowledge of others who have supported their children when someone in the family is seriously ill.

We appreciate that every person and every family will face what is happening in individual and unique ways. No family is like any other. It may be a child who is ill or a grandparent; it may be a parent… or it may be you. Supporting children under these circumstances is, quite simply, 'as big as it gets'.

The book is designed for parents, carers and professionals who are supporting children and young people facing the illness and possible death of someone important. It has sections about how to talk with children about what is happening, some possible reactions and emotions and how these may affect children and adults, and it looks towards the future. We mainly address the situation when it is a parent who is seriously ill; however, we also acknowledge that other important people in a child's life may be ill. Throughout, there are quotes from those who have had similar experiences and some creative ideas for ways to support children at this time.

Winston's Wish has supported families facing challenge and change throughout our history: we know that with the right support, children can find ways to live confidently with the worry and sadness. A time of great anxiety for all the family can also deepen the bonds between people.

The Winston's Wish Freephone National Helpline (08088 020 021) provides emotional support and a sounding board for those who are caring for children when someone is seriously ill, as well as information and guidance on how to support them and some links to local support.

WHAT IS HAPPENING

This book has been written so that children can feel resilient, strong and also confident enough to share the natural feelings of loss when someone they care about is seriously ill.

Some of the discussions and suggestions may feel almost unbearably challenging; the temptation will be strong to turn away and keep the reality away from children. If the illness is serious, it will already be affecting the family… even if it has not yet been talked about. Children have their antennae tuned for worry and stress affecting those close to them and will sense that something serious is happening.

Together, the ideas and activities we have included may act as an 'emotional insurance policy' and — as with having an insurance policy — having things in place will not make it more likely that the worst will happen. Hopefully, it will reassure parents and carers that there are tangible things that can help. Everything we have included is here because we know from our experience that it will help children and young people in the short or long term. There are no 'right' ways to negotiate what is happening but there are ways that can help children feel sufficiently secure and confident to weather the uncertainties that come when someone close is ill.

THE NATURE OF THE ILLNESS

We hope this book will be helpful, regardless of the illness in question. While cancer may be the serious illness that is first thought of – and the one that affects most people – there are other illnesses, such as multiple sclerosis (MS) or motor neurone disease (MND) that may also affect families. Much of the text assumes that there might be time to have conversations with children and to build memories for the future. It is also recognised that sometimes time is very short.

There are many organisations that can provide specific guidance for particular conditions: in this book, we will inevitably make some generalisations that might not be true for all illnesses.

Not so long ago, a diagnosis of advanced cancer, for example, would come with an expectation that someone would die. Treatments have been advancing for some conditions very rapidly and the timing of any deterioration in health is less predictable. People may unexpectedly enter remission when symptoms recede – or the illness may be cured. For this reason, the 'jigsaw' method of sharing information with younger children (see page 15) may be the most appropriate and gentlest approach to take.

WHO IS ILL?

PARENT

It will inevitably be very difficult for children and young people when a parent is seriously ill. If there is another parent or step-parent around, he or she may feel torn between caring for and worrying about the children and also the person who is ill. Sometimes, it may feel impossible to give everyone the attention they need.

For children, witnessing a parent's illness is very emotional; they want to be caring and supportive but sometimes they just feel cross and want the 'old' Mum or Dad back. The illness, as it progresses, intensifies the distress and the fear of the future without a loved parent.

This can be particularly complicated, emotionally, if the parent who is ill has been living apart from the family. A child or young person may feel they want to establish a connection while this is still possible, yet the ill parent may not have the capacity to be the person their child needs them to be.

Hardest of all, perhaps, is when a single parent is seriously ill. Not everyone has supportive family and friends on hand; it may be hard to be alone in supporting children while also being ill and thinking about a future in which there might be a need for different arrangements.

SIBLING

For children and young people, it can be exceptionally hard to witness the serious illness of a sibling. The child who is ill might be an admired big brother or an adored little sister. Equally, they may be the sibling who is perceived as the most annoying or infuriating — or the one who has been envied until now. The child who is ill will, understandably, take up the time and attention of their parent(s) but this can leave the other child/ren feeling left out at best or abandoned at worst. Children may feel that the illness of a sibling is their fault, because of something they did or something they thought, or they may worry that they too will become ill.

GRANDPARENT OR OTHER FAMILY MEMBER

Grandparents may have a very important place in their grandchildren's lives and hearts. While it is slightly more understandable for children that older people die, it can be very hard to watch someone precious become sicker. Grandparents may believe that children should be protected from knowing too much about their illness and put on a brave face in front of them – leading to confusion ('Granny says she's fine'). Many grandparents are involved in their grandchildren's everyday routines (for example, collecting from school) and changes to this can be disconcerting alongside the anxiety about the person.

TEACHER

Teachers hold special places in children's lives. If a class teacher, for example, becomes seriously ill, it will have a big impact on the class and on the school. Alongside the disruption of having alternative teachers is the difficulty of facing what may be the first experience a child has of knowing someone who is ill.

YOURSELF

You may be reading this because you are the person who is ill. It may feel overwhelming to read through – especially the sections later in the book when the messages to children may need to become more serious. You may be facing what is happening with the support of a close family and friendship circle or you may be feeling very alone. You will want to do everything in your power to protect your children from changes that may be coming. Trying to be emotionally available as a parent while you are feeling ill is never easy. We acknowledge your courage in preparing to talk with your children about what is happening. The Winston's Wish Freephone National Helpline (08088 020 021) is there to offer guidance and support.

The first version of this book was produced in association with a Channel 4 documentary series called 'The Mummy Diaries'. It showed our founder, Julie Stokes OBE, supporting five families when a mother was dying. We repeat our thanks to the families who so generously allowed us to share their stories.

Some parts of the programmes are available online (search for The Mummy Diaries Winston's Wish).

8

LIVING IN A DIFFERENT WAY

The reality of living with a serious illness, especially when the prognosis is not a good one, highlights the challenge of trying to live with uncertainty, manage difficult feelings and maintain hope. Involving children in such a complex emotional mix is daunting.

Increasingly, a diagnosis of something like cancer is more about a treatable illness than a terminal condition. A great many people recover from cancer; even those with a terminal prognosis are living longer. This makes timing conversations about the future more complicated.

Holding on to hope and living each day to the full inspires many people to feel they still have choices at a time when they could easily feel helpless and alone.

"I felt I was holding the worry and anxiety of separation, as well as trying to maintain family life. Having to get the children to school, do the shopping and housework as well as be 'Mum and Dad' when it came to managing tricky situations, like arguments or trouble at school, it was exhausting."
Jo

"I remember the day I decided to tell them that the cancer had returned. I was in the kitchen stirring spaghetti sauce. I wanted to keep moving that spoon for ever. When I stopped, I knew I would tell them something that would change their lives. If I didn't tell them, would it make it less real? I knew that wasn't an option and I dreaded the questions that could follow… but wanted to be both honest and hopeful. They deserved that at least. We cried, we laughed… we were in this together. This was the first day of the rest of our lives."
Jenni

TALKING WITH CHILDREN

DEALING WITH THE TRUTH – *See page 12*

AGES AND STAGES – *See page 13*

TELLING THE CHILDREN – *See page 14*

BALANCING HOPE AND HONESTY – *See page 16*

WHAT TO TELL AND WHEN – *See page 17*

CHOOSING THE RIGHT WORDS – *See page 17*

EXPLAINING CHANGE – *See page 18*

QUESTIONS CHILDREN MAY ASK – *See page 19*

There is an overriding instinct to protect children from things that will hurt them; it is only natural to want to shield people you love from news that will distress them. It is also only natural to want to avoid demanding and draining conversations at a time when your own resources may be very low. This makes you human. However, our experience shows us that children can live with and through tough times if they have the information and support they need to feel included.

Our suggestions are based on our experience of supporting thousands of families over many years but, inevitably, we have to generalise. You know your family best: there may be excellent reasons for doing things your way.

Telling children details about someone's illness is hugely emotive for all involved. Conversations like these will be difficult and upsetting for everyone, but afterwards parents and caregivers can feel relieved that they have been able to be honest and build a foundation of trust with their child.

> *"It's not a choice of whether they (children) are distressed but whether we know about it."*
> Grace H Christ

DEALING WITH THE TRUTH

Children have an ability to deal with the truth that adults often underestimate. Not knowing can often make children feel anxious and confused.

Pretending to children can make a bad situation even worse. The belief that children can be protected from knowing what is happening is mistaken: children almost always know 'something'. Partial or inaccurate information can be more worrying than the truth. If other people know about the illness, children may hear about what is happening from someone outside the family and this can lead to greater anxiety and lack of trust.

Some parents believe that if they don't talk about illness with their children, it will not touch them. However, if a parent cannot and does not acknowledge that someone is ill, they also cannot acknowledge the feelings, thoughts and responses that children will experience. Adults sometimes believe that as long as the experience is not given a name or is not discussed, children will go on with their lives as if nothing is happening. This is not the case.

We cannot stop children feeling sad, but if we talk about our feelings and give children clear information, we can support them in this sadness.

AGES AND STAGES

What you will tell your children about what is happening in your family will depend on many factors, one of which will be their level of understanding. Children build up an understanding of illness as they grow: for example it can be challenging for a child under five to grasp what it even means to be ill. They will need lots of repeated, simple, clear explanations of what is happening and what may happen.

Up to 10 years old, children may not be able to grasp all the implications of a life-threatening illness and will appreciate adults regularly checking their understanding of what is happening.

Teenagers will be able to reflect on what the illness will mean to them in the future: for example, that their parent or sibling may die and therefore will be absent from the big occasions of their life.

Children with learning difficulties or neurodevelopmental disorders (such as ASD) may find it particularly difficult to understand the changes that are happening to the person who is seriously ill and to the family and will benefit from straightforward language and clear explanations.

"I had begun to understand that she was dying and that I'd be the girl at school whose mother had died. But one day it hit me that this meant she'd never see my child – if I have children – or meet my future partner. It felt like I was grieving for all the times she would be missing in the future."
Verity

TELLING THE CHILDREN

WHO SHOULD TELL THEM?

Circumstances may be out of your control, but wherever possible it is best for children to hear what is happening from those they trust the most and with whom they feel most secure.

Whenever possible, it helps if the adult who is ill can, at least, be present when these conversations about the illness happen, even if they are too ill or emotional to lead the conversation. This helps a child feel involved and informed and avoids them wondering whether the person concerned knows about their illness.

This assumes, of course, that the person who is ill knows at least as much about what is happening to them as the child will; it is difficult to put a child in the position of having to 'keep this a secret from Grandpa.'

It also assumes that the family are all communicating and on the 'same side'.

THE TIME AND THE PLACE

There is, of course, no ideal time or place for these conversations; circumstances will conspire to disrupt the best plans. When possible, try and find a place and enough time for children to feel able to ask all their questions and to receive some reassurance... and then have some time for a bit of 'normal' family life (a game, a film, a pizza etc).

However, children's questions come at unpredictable times and sometimes there is a need to balance getting to school on time with having an important conversation. If it is not possible to answer then and there, it is important to acknowledge questions and then put them temporarily 'on hold' – making sure to return and answer them later.

In addition, family life does not happen in a vacuum and there may be other factors that will make this time even more challenging: for example, there may be imminent school changes or exams, the family pet may have died, money may be short, parents may be separating. These additional pressures and experiences of loss may make reactions even more intense.

BUILDING UP THE PICTURE

It can be helpful to think of the process as a little bit like putting together a jigsaw. Building the picture up in small steps may help you to feel more in control and you can adjust the steps to suit your child. Depending on how old children are or their level of understanding, these pieces may be added over minutes, days, weeks or months. The pace between stages will differ from child to child, due to their ability to understand as well as their willingness or reluctance to hear more information. Younger children may not need to have all the pieces from the beginning. For younger children, hearing that their loved one is ill may be all they can absorb at first. Even older children may not be able to handle being given too much information at one time or you may be able to tell them everything you know immediately – the complete jigsaw. Some young people describe getting stuck between wanting to know more and not wanting to upset their parents by asking questions. Not knowing can sometimes lead young people to make 'best guesses' or search online for information. Some guesses or information may be far from the truth and far more distressing and confusing.

Equally, there is a balance between being honest about what is happening and burdening a child over a long, sustained period with weighty information. It can be exceptionally hard for a young child to hold on to anxiety for a long time and to live in the shadow of always waiting for the death of the person they love.

Even when the end is inevitable, it can help younger children to have the information broken into smaller chunks so that the message about if and when a person is going to die becomes clearer over time: we explain this more on the following pages.

BALANCING HOPE AND HONESTY

Maintaining both **hope** and **honesty** is crucial at this time.

Children often surprise us with their capacity to absorb new experiences and difficult thoughts. Children need to understand that hope, fear, anger, sadness and intense love are all appropriate feelings when a person they care about is seriously ill.

Finding the right balance between sharing enough to make a child feel included and informed and not sharing too much too soon and quashing all hope is a tricky balancing act.

Our difficulty in talking with children often stems from our own anxieties and discomfort. Recognising our own fears, concerns and hopes for the future may be an important first step in feeling ready to involve children. We all seek to be in control so to be in a place of uncertainty and to allow your children to join you in that place takes great courage.

It is important for us to recognise that we are looking at the rest of our children's lives. If they are 'protected' from the truth, they may learn to distrust. There may be nothing more important in their lives at a time of immense change than continuing to trust the people they love – the person who is ill and the parent or family who will continue to care for them.

Every family is unique and different family members may have different approaches to discussing the illness and to involving the children in what is happening. It may help to talk to Winston's Wish or to one of the organisations listed on pages 52-53 to have some support in thinking these things through. Non-talkers won't magically transform into sharers but it will be helpful for the children if some agreement can be reached on involving them in what is happening and how this can be achieved.

WHAT TO TELL AND WHEN

What, when and how to have a conversation with children will depend on many things including:

• **The age and level of understanding of the children**

• **The nature of the prognosis – is the person likely to recover? If not, is there an idea of when they may die?**

• **Children's previous experience of loss**

There are three key things to tell children at the start:

• **That someone close to them is seriously ill**

• **The name of the illness**

• **The first piece of the 'jigsaw' of what may happen**

The first step may be to ask what they already think is happening; this helps you correct any confusion.

CHOOSING THE RIGHT WORDS

It is hard to find the right words on the spot, so you may prefer to rehearse what you want to say first and prepare some possible answers to questions. Try and use simple language that children will understand and use factual explanations. Children tend to worry more when things aren't clear. Sometimes books or websites may help explain a particular illness.

It is generally a good idea to tell children the name of the illness – they are likely to hear (or overhear) this name a lot and it helps them to begin to understand if they have the right name for the condition and not a confusing euphemism. Sometimes, it may be helpful to give more specific information: for example, not simply 'cancer' but 'a type of cancer called neuroblastoma.'

One explanation for a younger child might sound like this:

'Dad and I have something really important to tell you. You know that Dad has been feeling really ill and the doctor has been trying to find out what is wrong? Dad has been having some tests in the hospital and we now know that Dad has an illness called 'cancer'. This is a really serious illness – it's not like having a tummy ache from eating too much ice cream. The doctors who are looking after Dad will be giving Dad some special medicine and he may need an operation.'

It may be necessary to repeat an explanation many times while children gradually take in what is being said. Asking them questions to clarify that they have understood can be helpful.

EXPLAINING CHANGE

It is also worth explaining the other changes that may happen: for example, everyone may be more emotional than usual. Warn children that parents may seem distant or upset – or even grumpy – sometimes. Explain that this is not because of anything the children are doing: it is the effect of the worry and the medicine. If it is a sibling who is ill, at least one parent may need to be away from home for long periods while the sibling is being treated in hospital. Children may feel left out or overlooked for a while because the person who is ill needs lots of love and attention.

For example:

'While Josh is having the next part of his treatment, I'm going to need to stay at the hospital with him so he doesn't feel too frightened on his own. Dad will come and visit us there as much as he can but he will also be here every night for you. Because Dad also has to work, Granny will be coming to stay so everything keeps on going smoothly for you here.'

QUESTIONS CHILDREN MAY ASK

Children may have many questions, both when they hear about an illness affecting someone close, and in the weeks that follow. Encouraging questions – and taking them seriously – will reassure children and help them feel included.

They will appreciate their questions being answered simply and honestly, in words they can understand, and they will appreciate opportunities to ask more questions as time passes.

Equally, some children may find it hard to put their questions and fears into words and may need to be offered the answers without having to ask the questions.

If you don't know the answer – or need time to think about your reply – it is OK to say so. However, that should be followed by a promise to try to find out and then to come back with an answer when you have more information or when the time is right for you.

These are the sort of questions that may come up when children hear that someone close is seriously ill. Of course, questions and concerns are as individual as the person asking them… and our suggested replies are only meant as general guidance.

- **Who will look after me while xx is in hospital?**
  Because I need to be in the hospital as much as possible with xx, Aunty Jodie is going to be coming to stay for a few days. She's promised to bring that game you play at her house and to make her famous chocolate cake

- **What will happen to me if xx dies?**
  Life will be very different; we will miss xx and feel sad that they are not here but we will get through this together

- **Will you die too?**
  I have every intention of playing with your grandchildren, not simply your children! I will do all I can to remain healthy and go on looking after you

  It is really unlikely that I will die before you are grown up, but if I were to die, Martine and Peter would want you to live with them and their children so that you could keep going to the same school and still see your friends

- **Will I catch this too? Will I die?**
  You can't catch this illness. That's not how it works. It is really unusual and sad that xx has this illness – most people die when they are very old. I expect you will live to be 111!

- **Can I still go to football?**
  We'll do everything we can to keep things ticking over as normal. Jake's dad has offered you a lift every week – and he'll make sure you get something to eat beforehand. He says he's very good at making chips

- **Did I make this happen? Is it my fault?**
  Nothing you did or didn't do: nothing you said or thought – or didn't say or didn't think – made this happen. It's no one's fault

- **Do you still love me?**
  I love you with all my heart. Sometimes I will be so sad about what is happening that I forget to say it – but I will never ever stop loving you

"When I told the children their dad had gone to the hospice my five year-old, Finn, looked terrified and tearful. Some days later I learnt from his older sister that he had thought he might have to be adopted as Mum would now have to go and live with Dad in the hospice. Slowly I allowed myself to see the last year through his confused, bewildered eyes. I realised how little I had prepared and involved him in what was the biggest event of his life. All he knew was that family life was under threat; his playmate Dad couldn't play anymore. The older children knew a bit more, but as a family we were so busy protecting each other that we somehow stopped talking about the important stuff. We held a family meeting at the hospice. We cried. We laughed. We hugged. We were back on track. Together we could deal with the rollercoaster ride ahead."

Sharu

RIDING THE EMOTIONAL ROLLERCOASTER

FEELINGS, THOUGHTS AND BEHAVIOURS – *See page 22*

REACTING TO THE NEWS – *See page 23*

GIVE AND TAKE – *See page 23*

FEELING SECURE – *See page 24*

WHEN MORE HELP MAY BE NEEDED – *See page 26*

LOOKING AFTER YOURSELF – *See page 27*

FEELINGS, THOUGHTS AND BEHAVIOURS

Anyone facing the serious illness and anticipated death of someone they love experiences an enormous range of powerful emotions. Some of these are predictable: most children will feel sad, angry, confused and frightened. But there are so many more feelings and thoughts that will be experienced. Responding to these situations can prompt every single emotion in the world – and every single person will respond in their own unique way, because of their unique relationship with the person who is ill and because of their own inner resilience.

Sometimes, adults will say that children don't talk about their feelings. To be honest, it is hard for children to know how to put feelings into words beyond saying 'I feel sad that this is happening.' It may be through their behaviour (being very 'good' or disruptive, for example) that feelings may be displayed.

It is important to recognise that all feelings are valid and that thoughts can't be controlled. It is possible, however, to find ways of not hurting themselves or others while safely expressing those feelings. Some feelings can also find their way out in physical symptoms (e.g. head or tummy aches when there's no medical cause) or in a return to earlier behaviours (for example, bed-wetting).

All these feelings and responses are natural and common; children will appreciate knowing this and that they are understood, however they may be reacting. They will also appreciate help to manage these feelings when they seem overwhelming.

There are some activities that can help with powerful feelings and challenging behaviours on our website: visit winstonswish.org. Some of these can even be fun for both parents and children – humour can be an excellent antidote to fear and anxiety.

Children may show their response to what is happening in various ways. These are some of the common ones:

- Some children may cling very tightly, terrified that something will happen if they are not there
- Some children may withdraw from the person who is ill, unconsciously trying to become more independent
- Some children may feel sorry for themselves and then feel guilty
- Some children may try to be especially 'good', setting themselves impossibly high standards, as a way of bargaining with the illness, or as a way of trying to help their parents
- Some children may try and take on the role of adult
- Some children may try and take on the role of baby
- Some children may show frustration by being uncooperative, dismissive or angry at everything
- Some children may be quite 'hyper', laughing or shouting overexcitedly as a way to disguise their feelings
- Some children may experience physical symptoms, such as headaches or tummy aches or symptoms close to those of the person who is ill
- Some children may develop some particular behaviours (for example, washing their hands a lot) because they feel anxious and are feeling afraid of catching the illness
- Some children may return to some earlier behaviours (for example, thumb-sucking, temper tantrums, wakeful nights, bed-wetting)

REACTING TO THE NEWS

Children can respond very differently to the news that someone is seriously ill. They may be very distressed or be angry. However, children often have a natural response to huge news – they may 'jump' to something completely different in tone. For example, a very common response to something like *'I have something very sad to tell you – Granny is very, very ill...'* may be something like *'What's for tea?' 'Can I watch TV?' 'Can I play on my Xbox?'*

This does not mean that they don't care but it is sometimes hard for them to understand and respond to what has been said straight away. It can take children a while to express their fears and uncertainties after hearing the news and they may need some time to take in the enormity of what they have heard. Something everyday, like watching a familiar programme, makes them feel safe.

It is exceptionally hard to tell your children that someone they love is desperately ill. This person is usually someone you also love and care about and telling the children can make the news seem suddenly more real. Be prepared for your own reactions and call on any support from friends or family to help you.

> *"I would never have believed it possible for us to keep on keeping on while Mark was so desperately ill. There were times when all I wanted to do was pull the duvet over my head and cry. But someone always needed socks or supper or needed me to sort out an argument. They kept me going and I guess I kept them going and somehow, we are still afloat."*
> James

GIVE AND TAKE

Living with a serious illness in the family can be exhausting for everyone concerned. The mixture of uncertainty and hope can be draining and treatment can be tiring.

Warn your children that the people around them are likely to be emotional, distracted, even irritable. It's natural. This is a time in the family for some 'give and take' and for not taking things too personally. Everyone will be on a short fuse. Explain that it's not because of anything that they have done; they are still deeply loved and wanted.

Praise children who want to help and be involved but be careful not to overburden them. At the same time, show understanding to those children who need to be distracted and distanced from the day-to-day reality.

It may be particularly difficult for children if a sibling is seriously ill. Hand in hand with enormous love and concern can come a feeling of 'when is it going to be my turn for some attention?'

FEELING SECURE

At a time of great change, all children need reassurance and a sense of security amid the chaos.

For very young children this may come from sticking, as far as possible, to regular routines for meals and bedtime. When possible, caregivers who can provide additional hugs and attention if a parent needs to be focusing elsewhere can be a comfort.

School-age children will also value the reassurance of a normal routine. Maintaining school attendance and other activities they value (where this is possible) can help them feel safe. However, they will also value times when this is abandoned for something more important, such as:

- **A shared activity when 'Mum is feeling better tonight'**
- **A game that lasts right through to the very end and not just until teatime**
- **An important conversation that goes on past bedtime**

They will also appreciate reassurance about what might happen to them in the future. Even children of two healthy parents can feel reassured to know who would look after them if anything happened. (*'Mum and I have every intention of meeting your grandchildren one day: but in the unlikely event of something happening, Emma and Jez would look after you and love you.'*)

There are some activities that can help a child feel more secure during a time of change. Further details are on our website **winstonswish.org/abaig**

BIG AND SMALL

Children sometimes really struggle with separation from a parent who is having treatment or maybe having respite care in a hospice – or is needing to stay with someone who is in hospital. One idea to respond to this understandable 'separation anxiety' is to create a physical link between the child and the parent. One way of doing this is to have two matching items of different sizes, one 'Big' and one 'Small'. These could be, for example, two teddies, two giraffes, two racing cars, two keyrings. What matters is that there is a difference in size but 'Big' need not be huge (to avoid embarrassing an older child) and 'Small' can be quite tiny.

The idea is that the larger item represents the parent and the smaller item represents the child. When parent and child are together the two items snuggle up together on a shelf or in a drawer. On separation, the child takes 'Big' with them as a symbol of their parent and the parent takes 'Small' with them as a symbol of their child. And when parent and child are reunited, 'Big' and 'Small' go back to their shelf to share stories. This kind of message helps children to feel a close link to their parent. It can also be reassuring to know that the parent is also feeling apprehensive and wanting the link to their loved child.

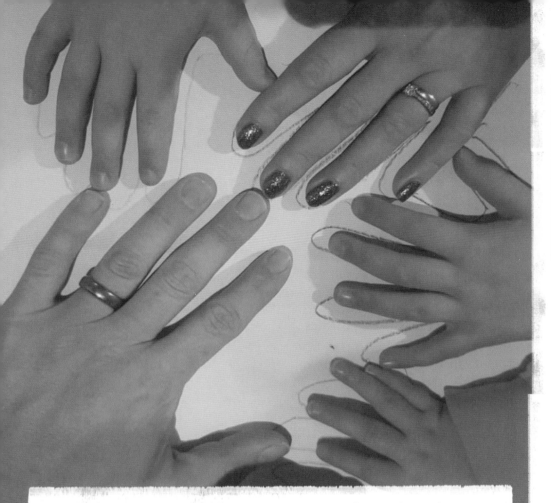

A very simple way of helping a child feel close to someone who is apart from them is to sew a secret kiss into the inside of a school jumper, for example. The child can press the kiss – with no one seeing – and feel the connection.

This can be taken further with a 'Splink' – a spot or dot which each person draws on their hand in pen. It may be a tiny dot or a larger heart or a kiss – these two 'Splinks' are pressed together on separation to demonstrate and consolidate the link between the two people and then can be pressed when apart to simulate the connection and the continuing love.

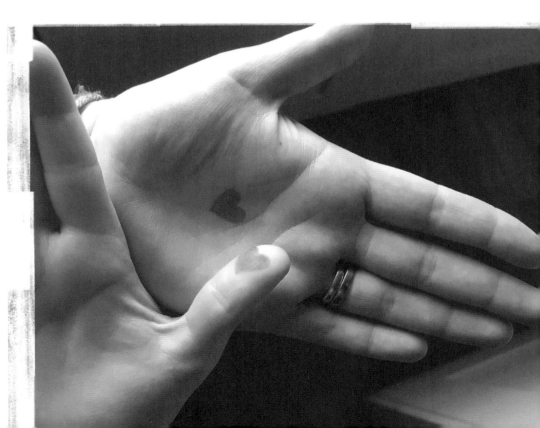

One simple way of helping a child feel close to family members who are away, for whatever reason, is to create a sheet of hand prints. Family members put one of their hands flat on a piece of paper (it may need to be a sheet of A3) with fingers touching and then draw around the outline of each hand with a different colour pen or crayon. A copy is made for each person who then puts it somewhere safe (for example, folded up in a pocket or school bag). When a child needs to feel close to their family (or indeed, when an adult does…), they take out their copy and place their hand on top of the outline they drew. They can then 'feel' or sense the fingers of the other people touching theirs and reminding them of their closeness.

WHEN MORE HELP MAY BE NEEDED

Most families can cope with a serious illness and, if they can talk about what is happening and how they feel about it, often surprise themselves by how well they cope.

Parents sometimes think that their children need professional help as soon as a serious illness is diagnosed. This may be because they feel helpless faced with children's reactions to the news. However, it is not always helpful to pass on the message that outside help from 'professionals' is necessary when a crisis happens. Most families somehow find the resources to support each other, even through the most difficult of times.

However, some difficulties may persist or begin to seriously affect a child's ability to withstand what is happening. The helplines on pages 52-53 can help determine if it is time to seek some additional support and where this might be most appropriately found.

LOOKING AFTER YOURSELF

When someone is seriously ill and may die, the caring adult can spend all their time and energy looking after other people. It seems important to be seen to 'cope'. Supporting children while someone important – maybe even you – is gravely ill is hugely demanding, both physically and emotionally. Parents can try so hard to protect their children that they can lose sight of their own need for support.

Sometimes adults feel they shouldn't get upset in front of children and children often say they want their parents to stop crying. While, of course, children are upset by a parent's distress, they need to see that the thing that is happening is, indeed, immense and is hurting everyone profoundly. However, while you may howl, you will then be able to make tea, drive to football training, play a game. Learning that huge emotions are appropriate and can be safely felt and expressed is so important and encourages children to risk opening up to their own feelings about what is happening.

Try to remember that 'Super Parents' don't exist and that you are doing the very best you can in exceptionally challenging circumstances. On aeroplanes, the safety demonstration reminds you to put on your own oxygen mask first before helping others. This is because you can't support others if you are overwhelmed yourself.

If at all possible, lean on others, be gentle on yourself and have a look at the sources of support on pages 52-53.

> *"Sometimes, I just had to walk outside and breathe. I had to see something that was growing – a tree or a flower. And then I could go back and pick it all up again."*
> Emma

"Somehow I felt as though I must carry on. After all, I wasn't sick myself and I suppose I thought 'men should cope'. I didn't have cancer and have to deal with all the treatments like Jane did. But I was breaking up inside while trying not to show it. Our GP was great. She asked all the right questions – we spoke regularly after that. I couldn't have come through this without her."
Mike

PREPARING FOR CHANGE

WHEN TREATMENT IS NECESSARY – *See page 30*

EXPLAINING SIDE EFFECTS – *See page 30*

IF TREATMENT IS NOT SUCCESSFUL – *See page 31*

CARE WITH WORDS – *See page 32*

TELLING FAMILY AND FRIENDS – *See page 33*

VISITING THE HOSPITAL OR HOSPICE – *See page 34*

STAYING AWAY FROM HOME – *See page 35*

WHEN RECOVERY IS UNLIKELY – *See page 36*

WHEN DEATH IS IMMINENT – *See page 37*

PREPARING FOR THE FUTURE – *See page 38*

The following sections follow a possible scenario when the person who is ill gradually becomes more sick and eventually dies.

It is important to repeat the point that many grave illnesses are treatable and that even at a late stage, recovery is a possibility.

The suggested content of conversations follow the 'jigsaw' idea we explained on page 15; building on the idea of adding pieces to build up the picture and, if it becomes necessary, gradually making the content of these conversations a little darker in tone.

WHEN TREATMENT IS NECESSARY

If there is a chance that treatment will work, the message can be fairly positive:

'Because of the illness that Grandma has, the doctors are going to do an operation to see if they can fix what is wrong with her. She will have to stay in hospital for a while but the doctors believe there's a good chance this will make her better.'

Children will appreciate involvement, such as writing cards or sending some flowers or sweets to the person who is ill.

EXPLAINING SIDE EFFECTS

Children will respond more confidently if they have forewarning of the impact of some treatments, for example, for cancer. Both the illness and some treatments may change a person's appearance. They may lose weight, lose their hair or have tubes connected. They will definitely feel very tired and may be sick during treatment. This can be frustrating for children who want the 'normal'/healthy person back and who will find it hard to understand why the person doesn't feel able to play games.

'The doctors have decided that it will help Mum if they give her some strong medicine to try to treat the cancer. It is called chemotherapy/radiotherapy/etc. Although the hope is that this medicine will make Mum better in the long run, it's such strong medicine that it may make her seem more ill at first. She may be very tired and very sick. It's possible that her hair may begin to come out. These changes are happening because the medicine and Mum's body are working hard to try to make her better.'

Adults and older teenagers will understand that sometimes treatment can make you ill in the short term for the longer-term good. For younger children, lots of reassurance that the doctors are trying to help the ill person may be necessary.

'Dad's medicine tries to make sure he doesn't have much pain, but it is really strong medicine and sometimes it makes Dad feel woozy. He might say things that come out in a funny way – that's just the effect of the treatment.'

'When people are ill, they often do very little because their bodies aren't working well and are concentrating all their energy to cure the illness. Carl doesn't need to eat much or do much and spends most of his time sleeping – but he knows you are here and that you love him. He loves you too.'

Preparing children in advance of any possible changes can help to reassure them that the person is still their important person, even though they may look different.

If the person is away from home during treatment, it may help to prepare the children in advance of a return home by taking a photo of the person receiving treatment or by having a brief video chat. Some changes are not necessarily the result of treatment; children can be confused, for example, about why their very blonde mum returns home after a prolonged hospital stay with mousy brown hair.

IF TREATMENT IS NOT SUCCESSFUL

It may be that there will be a need for further treatment or a change of treatment. This is time for another piece of the picture:

'The doctors and nurses are all trying so hard to make Grandma better and it is a real shame that the operation didn't help as much as they hoped. But the illness she has is difficult to treat. The doctors are having a think about what treatment to try next, but right now we're not really sure what will happen. We have an appointment with the chief doctor – the consultant – on Friday.'

"My dad has cancer and he was in hospital for a long time. When he finally came home, he was still really sick. I had to help him up the stairs because he was so weak. It was strange because he had always been so big and strong – he could lift me up with one hand. It scared me."
Dani

CARE WITH WORDS

Children will appreciate hearing the right words for what is happening: having a name for a thing makes it easier to begin to understand that this is a new thing to face and to understand.

Sometimes people are anxious about even saying something like cancer or motor neurone disease and tend to use confusing terms like 'The Big C'. Or there may be a temptation to play down the illness by describing it as 'having a poorly tummy', for example. Describing the illness that may lead to the death of someone important as 'being poorly' can lead to distress and fear in the future when they are themselves 'a bit poorly'.

'Dad's illness has got a name – it's called cancer and Dad's cancer seems to be affecting his lungs. It is making Dad really ill. This isn't like when you are out of breath after running across the playground or when someone has to use an inhaler for asthma. This is a serious illness that is making Dad's lungs struggle to work properly.'

Another challenge with language is the way that some people, and the media in particular, have taken to referring to the experience of having a life-threatening illness as being engaged in a battle. Those with the illness are encouraged to 'fight' it, to 'stay strong'. If they do not recover, people may talk about having lost the 'battle'. While a positive attitude may be helpful to both the person who is ill and those around them, this kind of language can have an unintended consequence. It implies that if someone fails to recover they didn't try hard enough, weren't brave enough, didn't love their children enough. If this is the language surrounding the child, it can increase distress to hear of a loved one being engaged in a fight – and be distressing to have them depicted as a loser.

"If one more person tells me I'm a fighter when actually I'm a coward, I don't know what I'll do. Of course I want to live. I'm doing the best I can. Don't make me feel I'm in some sort of video game and you're judging me on my score of vanquished baddies."
Anne

TELLING FAMILY AND FRIENDS

Family and friends will also be keen to offer support to you and your children. You may want their support and presence – or you may need time to yourselves.

It may help to have a few sentences in your mind to answer questions from well-meaning people. For example:

'Yes, Danny is very ill. We are all in shock. I'm sure you'll understand if I don't want to say any more at the moment…'

'Our darling Annie is in the children's hospice now and we don't think she will come home again. We're just trying to get our heads around it…'

'Thank you so much for offering help. I'm not thinking straight right now but I am grateful…'

33

VISITING THE HOSPITAL OR HOSPICE

Sometimes, the person who is ill is apprehensive about having children visit. Frequent concerns are around whether the children will be distressed or frightened. Often there is a feeling that 'I don't want them to remember me like this.' Sometimes, it is because the person who is ill can't quite bear the pain and poignancy of seeing their loved children or grandchildren.

There are big benefits to the children concerned in including them at all stages: for example, it helps them to understand what is happening and it reduces the fear that the person has altered out of all recognition. Sometimes, a child will question if the person loves them if they are not allowing them to visit. They will feel excluded at a time when they most need to feel included. With detailed preparation in advance to reduce the elements that are unknown, children can manage most situations. Having a clear idea in advance means they can concentrate on the most important thing – the person who is ill.

'Mum is in a room with three other beds in it – sometimes there are people in all these beds but yesterday there was just one other person. Mum is in the bed by the window so she can see the treetops and the clouds – she likes that. She looks just like Mum – but also very tired and rather pale. She'll probably be wearing that blue nightie I gave her for Christmas. She has a table on wheels beside her with enough flowers to open a flower shop. Your cards are all around her. There'll also be some equipment beeping away in the background and Mum has a tube in her arm that they use to give her medicine.'

Visits need not be long to be important to both sides. It may help children to have a task to perform, such as to fill up the flower vases, offer a drink, draw a picture that can stay behind when they leave. Children's hospices usually find creative ways of making siblings' visits enjoyable.

On the other hand, sometimes children just cannot bear the idea of visiting. This can be very upsetting for the person who is ill, but it may be more upsetting for all concerned to insist. To maintain the connection, other ideas are needed: phone calls, cards, photos of the cat doing something silly, suggested music tracks, home-made biscuits.

Even the very briefest of visits can be meaningful and help prevent a child, in the future, feeling guilty or regretful that they did not visit. A quick dash in with a flower or magazine and back out to a supporting friend or family member can make all the difference in the world.

"She couldn't bear to see Euan like that and I couldn't force her. It was breaking his heart though. My friend helped her make a card which she just managed to hand over to him and then Val took her down to the hospital shop to buy some sweets and a paper for Euan. She gave it to him (and some of her sweets) and hurried back out again. It meant all the world to him – and, later, it meant all the world to her too."
Jess

STAYING AWAY FROM HOME

Sometimes it is felt necessary or desirable for children to stay somewhere else when someone is seriously ill. For example, this may be because their parent(s) are trying so hard to cope with the extra pressures and demands that looking after someone can bring and have little time to give attention to their children. While this will be done for the best of reasons, it may feel to children as if they are being punished in some way. It may make them wonder again whether they have been naughty, whether they have caused the illness and therefore been sent away. They may be very anxious and distressed if they are excluded from what is going on at home.

Equally, it can be a relief to have some time away, to have some loud fun with cousins, for example, rather than tiptoeing around in silence at home. Just a short time of being 'normal' can help children withstand what is happening.

'I've arranged for you and Zach to stay with Granny for four days. As you know, Dad is really sick right now and I need to spend all my time getting his special meals and medicine and helping him wash. He also needs me in the night as the coughing can be quite bad then so I don't get much sleep. Granny has offered to help out, so this week you will go and stay at her house for a few days and then she will come and stay with us all here for a few days. Everything else like school and swimming will stay the same. And I will ring you every morning and evening to let you know how things are going.'

The important thing is to work out ways to stay in touch: regular visits, phone calls, video chats or texts all help children to continue to feel included and involved.

WHEN RECOVERY IS UNLIKELY

The pieces can to be added to the jigsaw while treatment continues. For example:

'The doctors have tried to make Mum better – they have tried every treatment but, unfortunately, none of them seem to be working. Sometimes this happens with this particular illness; not all the treatments work all of the time.'

If it becomes clear that the person who is ill is unlikely to survive for much longer, it is time for the hardest conversation of all. The key points to convey are that the doctors have tried, that it is no one's fault and that the person does not have long to live.

'You know how Ellie has been having all these treatments for her illness and that I told you that none of them had worked? Well, I talked to her doctor today and she said that there is nothing else they can do to make Ellie better now. She thinks that Ellie doesn't have much longer to live and that's why she's sleeping so much of the time.'

Older children may be able to handle more uncertainty and be able to cope with more information.

'The doctor says that Dad's cancer has got much worse and we now know that he will die. We hope we will have a few more months together but we don't think he will be alive for your next birthday. He may seem OK to begin with and the doctors will do their best to make sure he's not in pain.'

As an important person in a child's life becomes more ill, it may be that the children instinctively ask fewer questions; they are guarding themselves from facing the reality of what will happen next. This makes it particularly important that the adults around them keep the information flowing and keep checking what is being understood.

Sometimes, a 'protection racket' springs up: parents don't want to distress their children, children try and protect their parents and no one ends up sharing their fears and concerns. Sometimes, everyone knows that a person is going to die, but no one acknowledges this… and everyone ends up feeling isolated. Even the saddest truths may be better than the uncertainty of not knowing what is happening.

WHEN DEATH IS IMMINENT

When it is clear that the person will die shortly, it is time for the last pieces of the jigsaw.

'You know I told you that the treatment Mum has been receiving has not worked and that she does not have long to live? Well, we now understand that she may die within the next few days. She will probably be asleep almost all of that time. We will be able to say our goodbyes and spend some precious time with her before she dies. It's possible that she can still hear us but she won't be able to talk. Soon her breathing will slow right down and then there will come the moment when her heart will stop and she will die."

The last days of life will inevitably be heartbreakingly sad for all concerned. Yet, with the right help and support, children will be able to look back on these days as being full of love and closeness.

37

PREPARING FOR THE FUTURE

It can be exhausting both being the person who is ill and being the one who is providing care and concern. However, if survival is unlikely, there are a few things that can be put in place that may help a child in the future. These include some practical tasks and some tasks around building memories for the future.

A helpful resource for all parents – not simply those who are terminally ill – is called 'Plan If'. Since at least 1 in 4 parents die suddenly, for example, through an accident or something like a heart attack, it is important that things are in place that will ease the experience of bereavement should the unthinkable happen.

Plan If divides ideas into things that can be put in place this week, this month or this year. More details can be found on the website (www.planif.org.uk) developed by the Childhood Bereavement Network.

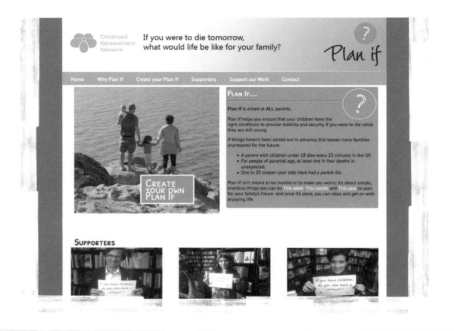

THIS WEEK

- Making a will
- Appointing guardians
- Checking life insurance
- Creating a contact list

THIS MONTH

- Sorting financial affairs
- Digital assets
- Writing letters for the future
- Listing important people to maintain contact with

THIS YEAR

- Planning end-of-life care
- Donating organs and tissue
- Writing cards for future occasions
- Recording family history
- Compiling a 'Keeping things ticking over' manual

WRITING INTO THE FUTURE

There are some ideas which can have particular value and meaning if life is likely to be cut short. One of these is writing a letter to be read by children in the future. This is a tough yet rewarding thing to do: we have yet to meet anyone who has achieved it dry-eyed. Having such a letter, if a parent dies, can be an enormous comfort to a child and will always be treasured.

You don't need to be a brilliant writer to write such a letter. The key things to include are:

- **that you love them**

- **that you have been so privileged to be their parent**

- **that you are proud of them and know they will have an amazing future**

- **a recognition of some of their special qualities (kindness, perseverance, humour etc)**

- **regret that you won't be around to see what happens**

- **and a bit more love…**

It is also possible to record a piece to be viewed after your death. There are several services providing this, including *Record Me Now: Dead Social* and *If I Should Die*. This may be more appropriate if, for example, your child may not be able to read and/or understand your letter.

The only risk of letters such as these is that children may feel they have been given a set of instructions which need to be followed out of respect for the letter writer. Sometimes, such letters may refer to 'graduation' or 'marriage'; if such references are included, it is important to emphasise that whatever future choices children make are respected so they do not feel they have let the author down if they do not go to university, marry or have children.

The Plan If website has some great examples, for example from the writer Caitlin Moran and from the film *Billy Elliot*. The following pages show examples written by a single mother to her eight-year-old child and a father to his 17-year-old son.

This letter is from a single mother writing to her eight-year-old daughter Sarah. This letter had been written and filed away for 11 months. It was given to Sarah by her guardians, Susan and Dan, after her mother died and is now kept safely in her memory box:

Dear Sarah

I am so, so, so, so sorry that you are reading this letter — I hoped you would never have to. I wish with all my heart that I was still alive and still with you and we could go on with our lives together.

You have been the most wonderful, marvellous, amazing daughter!! I have loved every single moment of being your mother and feel immensely proud to have you as my daughter.

I know you will be feeling sad. Desperately sad. You've had too much death in your life — too much death of those you love — Grandpa, Bramble, Shelly-Hamster and the other animals. It's not fair on you — but please know that it's not something you are causing, it's just terribly unfair.

Please don't be afraid to love people in the future. It's the best thing to do! I wish I could be there now to comfort you. Isn't it sad that the one person who might be able to make it better is the one person who's made it worse? Cry all you can. Hug Big Ted and Liddly and sob. Hug humans too. Susan and Dan, and Grandma are all good for hugs. And when the time comes to stop crying — and it will — please stop. Don't feel bad about stopping, it's the right thing after a while. I hope you won't stay sad for a long time... remember the happy times instead.

Remember all the good times. All the fun. All the love. We've had such good, good times, haven't we? Times at home with pets and toys and water fights and snuggles on the sofa. Times away on holiday. Times just travelling along in the car, chatting.

Talk about me a lot! Not in a sad way but just keep remembering some funny and ordinary things — and then talk about them. I've written some memories down but I know you'll think of loads more.

Some days won't be as good as others. You might feel angry, lonely, afraid, confused. Talk to other people about how you feel. There are two things that worry me... one is that you might feel uncomfortable about some of the times when we've argued. Sarah, listen to me... please forget this. It's not important. All that's important is how much we love each other (and we really, really do) and all the goodness and joy we have had between us.

The other thing that concerns me is your occasional lack of confidence and belief in yourself — like when you say you don't want to do something because you might fail. Please remember that you are a unique and amazing individual. And you are full of loving ways. I love your creativity and enthusiasm. For my sake, please remember that you are wonderful — all the best of things rolled up in one special daughter.

I hope the rest of your life is everything you want it to be. Tough stuff can and will happen and I know you will find ways to survive, be strong and learn. Susan and Dan will be great people to grow up with, lean on, rely on (and argue with sometimes!). I hope you will have a group of special friends to trust and eventually someone special to love. I hope you find work that satisfies and nourishes you. I hope your dreams come true — whatever they may be. And on the special days of your life, remember me and know that I am so proud of you and I am surrounding you with my love.

It has been wonderful to share these years with you. I'm so sorry I couldn't stay. I'd have done anything to be able to. My love for you is so strong — nothing can break it, certainly not something as insignificant as death. My love will surround you, protect you, nourish you and support you all the days of your life.

Remember me, love me, love others, love yourself — I love you forever.

Mum x x x x x x

This letter is from a father to his 17-year-old son as he started a tough treatment regime. He gave it to him with a memory box (see page 45). It had a photo of the two of them together on the lid and was filled with photos from holidays and parties, certificates of their sporting achievements, grandfather's cufflinks and his favourite aftershave.

Dear Ross

This is the hardest letter I've ever written. There are so many things I want you to know — it's difficult to know where to start.

I think the most important thing for you to always remember is that you have a dad who thinks you are THE VERY BEST son a father could have! I have known you for 17 years and even though we don't always agree on everything (especially your terrible taste in music!), I am so proud to have you as my son.

Right now, things don't look too great in terms of my health. The doctors think that I'm unlikely to get better, even with the strong chemo, so my future is uncertain.

I feel so very angry that I may not be able to share the rest of your growing up years. I have had a lot of time to think lately and I realise that life is for living so I hope we will make the most of our time together and make some memories. Maybe we could start you off driving?

Somehow, life goes on and we will remain close to each other — wherever we might be.

I'll always love you, never, ever forget that.

Dad x x

LITTLE BOX OF BIG THOUGHTS

Writing down special memories and thoughts about the future can create a unique and lasting reminder for children of a shared bond. This isn't an activity to be undertaken only when a parent or grandparent is seriously ill; the little box can be a lasting symbol of a bond between people. It can also be a simpler task if writing a letter seems too big to undertake.

There are several ways to go about preparing such a resource: some people use special boxes with some suggested 'prompts', others use sticky notes or coloured paper and keep the thoughts in a jam jar or in a memory box. Initially it seems a daunting prospect, but it is a project that can be added to at any time – not completed all at once.

You could start with some simple phrases such as:

- *I love you because…*
- *I feel proud when you…*
- *I hope that…*
- *You make me laugh when…*
- *One favourite memory I have is…*
- *One thing I notice about you is…*
- *Thank you for…*
- *I wish…*
- *When we're not together, the thing I miss most about you is…*

'MUDDLING THROUGH' MANUAL

Sometimes, parents who are facing the end of their own lives can feel overwhelmingly anxious about what will happen to their children in the future. It may be that they are surrounded by loving family and friends and have a remaining parent or carer closely involved in their day-to-day care. Or it may be a single parent who is trying to secure their children's futures. Parents have told us that they felt a tiny bit more in control if they noted down some helpful hints about everyday routines for those who are – or will be – looking after their children. This really need not (and should not) be prescriptive. It won't matter if a child gets the 'wrong' sandwich filling or if swimming club is forgotten. Muddling through is a way for the surviving family to support each other as they find new ways to do things.

However, the security of familiar routines and practices can help grieving or anxious children weather some of the early days. Information about things like: friendships and any potential challenges (*'Amy has never liked staying over at Ella's because of their dog…'*); clubs and groups (*'Sam has football on Monday and Jake's dad will take him and bring him back'*); preferred foods or hairstyles etc can all act as background reassurance that this huge, huge loss can be lived through.

> *"When we told her that Anji had to go back to hospital, she wanted to know who was going to do her hair in the morning. At the time I thought it was a funny question but she seemed calmer when Anji explained that she'd show me how to do a plait the way she likes it – and also that I might have unexplored skills in that area! It set the tone for my daughter and me finding our own ways of doing things…"*
> Jai

MEMORIES – BUILDING THEM NOW

Depending on how long a time there is after diagnosis, the age of the children involved and the stamina of the person who is ill, there may be an opportunity to create lasting memories. These may be captured in photographs and videos and children appreciate the opportunity to hear their important person's voice, for example, reading a favourite story. If the person who is ill has a favourite perfume or aftershave, it can form a lasting reminder of their bond for children. Now is the time to apply it regularly so that a drop or two on a pillow at night can create a link to the person who may be in hospital or a hospice and maintain that link, at a deep level, after they have died.

There will be people or places in family photos that only the person who is ill can identify — labelling these can create a rich resource for children. It can also be hugely valuable if someone can create a family tree – especially if the person with all the knowledge is the person who is ill.

As a child grows up without this important person, they may become more aware of gaps in their memories. It can help to build up memories with stories about the person who died, looking at photographs and personal items and talking about them. Supportive family and friends can help paint a real and vivid picture of the person who is dying or who has died by sharing their own stories and memories: sometimes it helps to jot down the start of a story on a Post-it to be shared at a later date (**'Ask me about the time your dad got stuck on the school roof'**). In this way, the person's death does not come to define them; children will be able to think and talk about their life.

The Winston's Wish website shop (shop.winstonswish.org) has some resources to support the sharing of family stories and history. These include:

Dad & Me and **Mum & Me,** interactive journals to inspire any parent and child to have a great time getting to know each other better. Guided prompts take the parent and their child on an enjoyable journey of discovery about family times, holidays, friendships, growing up, school and much more. Spaces to draw, doodle and write make these books easy to use — a gift with a lasting legacy.

Dear Mum and **Dear Dad**
These journals are full of around 60 questions carefully designed to inspire every parent to tell his or her personal story. They help parents capture the stories and memories that make up who they are and can be completed by any parent who wants to build a record for their children.

"When Dad was still able to talk, he gave me this box with things in. He'd kept so many odd things, like cinema tickets and all the Fathers' Day cards I'd made for him. He said it would help me never forget things we did together."
Carl

MEMORY BOX

When someone in the family is seriously ill, memories of shared times can be comforting and can help children feel close to the person. One way of doing this is to start building a memory box.

Children can also be helped and encouraged to add to the memory box themselves if the person dies.

STEP 1 Fill your memory box with items that are about times spent together or things you have shared. These can include things like a watch, a tie, a scarf, some jewellery. You could include some photographs and cards from birthdays. Some perfume or aftershave? How about a pair of glasses or a favourite CD?

STEP 2 Try and make sure that the things in your box have a story or memory attached

STEP 3 It can really help if the person creating the box can write a label for each item to jog memories

STEP 4 Some children like to keep their boxes private, others like to show them to family and friends; it's totally up to you

TOOLKIT

• A box (you could buy one from the Winston's Wish website or you could make your own out of something like a shoebox)

• Some things that trigger memories of times shared, for example: a piece of jewellery, an item of clothing, a favourite book, shells from a holiday, tickets from a day out

• Pens, stickers, glitter etc — if you'd like to personalise your box

"Dad and me once went to watch our team play. The ticket and the programme and a photo of us there all help to remind me of what a great day it was..."
Ollie

"It took a long time to accept that things were going to change. There was such a strong urge to protect them from anything sad. And yet, once we'd started talking about it everything became easier. I'd say: nothing is going to feel quite the same but this is our 'new normal'."
Paul

LOOKING AHEAD

THE ROLE OF SCHOOLS – *See page 48*

SCHOOL SUPPORT – *See page 49*

AN ALTERED FUTURE – *See page 51*

WHERE TO SEEK FURTHER SUPPORT – *See page 52*

THE ROLE OF SCHOOLS

School plays a familiar and routine part in children's lives. At a time of uncertainty and challenge, many children want to keep attending school because it gives them a sense of stability and security in the middle of the chaos. Some will see school as a place to pause thinking about what is happening for a few hours. Others may feel too anxious, confused and upset to join in with school activities or be shy of being upset in front of other children. Some may find it too much of a challenge to go to school at all. This may be because they don't want to leave their family and are anxious about the person dying when they are not there; others may want to be at home to be a support to their family. All of these reactions are natural.

TALKING WITH THE SCHOOL

It can be very helpful to inform the school as soon as possible when an illness affecting someone important to a child becomes serious. This gives the school a chance to prepare both to respond to an individual child and also to consider how to communicate with and support the whole school. Talking it through also provides an opportunity to agree how the information about a particular situation is handled. Schools will strive to respond to individual choices but, by and large, it is worthwhile for staff to know what is happening and to communicate this with other students, where and when appropriate.

It may feel very difficult to talk to the school but the more that teachers know about what is happening and how things are at home, the more they are able to help. School staff will want to understand how the school can make a positive response. They may appreciate a conversation along the lines of:

'As you know, our family is going through a really tough time at the moment. You may have heard that Katy's dad is back in the hospice. It's looking as if he may only have a short time to live. It's been a huge shock and we are all still all over the place. Katy is keen to stay at school but a bit anxious about what it will be like. I wanted to have a word about what sort of support she will be able to have. She wondered if she would be able to talk to {named member of staff} if things get too much? We will want to take her out of school when her dad reaches the end of his life so she can say goodbye.'

SCHOOL SUPPORT

Schools and teachers have such an important role for children. One of the most valuable things they can do is simply to acknowledge what is happening: children tell us that having a teacher say: 'I'm really sorry to hear your dad's back in hospital' makes a big difference.

Ensuring that all members of the school staff know what is happening can help them provide support for a child facing the death of someone important. This is easier at primary or first school level when a class teacher can keep eyes and ears open for signs of distress and requires more communication at secondary or high school level when more people need to remember.

'You may have heard that the father of Katy in Year 4 is back in the hospice. He hasn't got long to live. Katy knows this and is, of course, very worried and upset. She may need some extra support both now and, of course, after he dies. Her grandpa has come to stay because Katy's mum is spending a lot of time with her dad.'

Winston's Wish has a **Schools Information Pack** and a **Strategy for Schools** which include guidance on discussing a death or serious illness affecting a school community, ideas for lesson plans, sample letters for parents and/or governors. These can be obtained by contacting the Winston's Wish Freephone National Helpline on 08088 020 021 where guidance and information on handling individual circumstances can also be.

"We had two children in the school whose mother was dying; she had helped out in the classrooms and at lunchtime so all the school knew her. It was so hard, not only to support these children, but to manage the anxiety of the other children about their mothers or fathers dying too. It was really good to talk this through with the helpline."
Helen Deputy Head Teacher

FOR CHILDREN AND YOUNG PEOPLE

- Think through how you will answer any questions; it might help to practise this with your family. For example, you might feel you can only say something like:
  'Yes, my brother is very ill. I don't want to talk about it just now.'

- Or you may want to share a little more about what is happening and how you are feeling, for example:
  'My mum has got an illness called cancer. It makes her very sick and she has to go to the hospital a lot for treatment and then I have to go to my gran's for a few days. I am scared about what is happening. I just can't believe it.'

- It may help to ask your friends to look out for you and have a word with a teacher if some people are being too inquisitive or unkind

- Talk with your teacher about what to do if it all becomes a bit too much: for example, have a few minutes 'time out', a walk around the playground, a glass of water

- You may feel as if all your concentration is on the person who is ill. Try and tell someone, for example:
  'I just can't focus on sums right now. I am so worried about my dad: what if he gets worse and I'm not there with him?'

- It is natural to feel a huge and confusing range of emotions – and also to feel almost numb. Be gentle on yourself

- Try and get hold of some 'Stepping Stones' cards – they help you with ideas for talking to your parent or carer, teacher and friends when someone is seriously ill (see page 54)

FOR TEACHERS AND OTHER SCHOOL STAFF

- Acknowledge to the child what is happening, for example:
  'I'm so sorry to hear about your gran, how is she today?'

- Help the child to think through how they will respond to questions

- Give the class/school some guidance on what to say: for example:
  'It's a very tough time for Alex. Think about how you can be kind… you might want to say: "I'm sorry your mum is so ill." Alex might not feel able to reply but will appreciate if you understand that and still include him in games.'

- Discuss with the child what they would like to do if it all becomes a bit overwhelming. This might include a 'Time Out' card (when they can have a few minutes out of the classroom) or an 'Emotional First-Aid Kit' of strategies. Visit **winstonswish.org/abaig** for downloads

- Consider the planned curriculum for the next weeks and, ideally, next few terms. Lesson content involving death or dying (for example, some set books) may be tough for a child to handle. They will appreciate having some warning in advance and the chance to choose how to be involved

- Keep an eye out for other children in the class or school who may also have someone ill or someone who has died

AN ALTERED FUTURE

Reading through this booklet may have been almost unbearably difficult. If it is you who is ill, reading the last few pages may have been almost impossible.

However, facing your worst fears may make it easier to begin to discuss what is happening and what will happen with those close to you, including your children. Sharing feelings and thoughts, talking things over and building memories are laying down crucial strengths that children will call upon for the rest of their lives.

It may help to think of this tough time as 'Bear Hunt' territory: you can't go over it, you can't go round it, you can't go under it, you have to go through it. It helps to hold hands while you do.

In time, children will remember the person who lived – rather than what happened when they were ill and died.

Above all, we hope that the ideas and suggestions in this book will help to make it possible for your family to live through and beyond what is happening.

With the right help and support, children will find their way to an altered future, one which is resilient and fulfilling, and enriched by having shared this profound experience with those close to them.

The spirit of family life and the love between family members are stronger than any illness.

WHERE TO SEEK FURTHER SUPPORT

You may feel that you need the support of those who understand some of the special circumstances involving the serious illness and possible death of someone close. If you are finding it hard to reach out to family and friends, consider contacting one of the organisations that can offer listening and support to those who are struggling. This list concentrates on organisations that support families when someone is seriously ill, and many contacts below are about supporting a child when someone has cancer. There are other organisations that can help when a person is seriously ill with other conditions, for example MS, MND, MSA, AIDS.

HOSPICE SUPPORT

Adult hospices

Most hospices have at least begun to explore how to support children when someone is gravely ill; many have long-established services. In some places, this may be through individual work with trained staff and/or attendance at a group with other children. The person who is ill may not need to be attending the hospice for children to receive support.

In some hospices, these same groups continue after a death; in others, children may be invited to a new bereavement group.

The care team or allocated Macmillan nurse can make a link to the appropriate hospice or the website of Hospice UK has a searchable map. **www.hospiceuk.org**

Children's hospices

Children's hospices offer individual and/or group support to siblings of the child who is gravely ill. As with adult hospices, this may be through attendance at one group, both before and after the death of a sibling, or may be in separate groups.

There is a searchable directory of local support through the website of **www.togetherforshortlives.org.uk**

HELPLINES FOR ADULTS WHEN SOMEONE IS SERIOUSLY ILL

The **Winston's Wish** Freephone National Helpline offers guidance, information and support to anyone supporting a child when someone important is seriously ill.

www.winstonswish.org

08088 020 021 (Monday to Friday, 9am to 5.30pm)

The **Macmillan** Support Line, staffed by trained experts, offers people with cancer and their loved ones practical, clinical, financial and emotional support. They have five services, accessed through the main number.

www.macmillan.org.uk

0808 808 00 00 (Monday to Friday)

Cancer information and support (9am - 8pm)
This team answers each call, provides emotional and practical support, or can just listen if someone needs to talk. They will help find the best support, which could be through speaking to one of the specialist teams listed below, finding relevant resources online or support in local areas.

Cancer information nurse specialists (9am - 8pm)
This team of experienced cancer nurses uses their clinical skills to provide and talk through specialist information on symptoms and diagnosis, treatment, living with cancer, palliative care and end of life.

Financial guidance (9am - 5pm)
Financial specialists are available to provide help with finances, offering guidance in areas such as mortgages, insurance, pensions, future planning and more.

Welfare rights (9am - 8pm)
Providing information on benefits and grants that may be available and also on NHS health costs.

Energy advice (9am - 5pm)
Energy specialists can help to source funding if utility bills are a problem for someone with cancer.

The **Marie Curie** Support Line is for anyone living with or caring for someone who has a terminal illness, to offer practical information and emotional support whatever the situation. The Support Line can provide support in over 200 languages through a third-party interpreter.

www.mariecurie.org.uk

0800 090 2309 (Monday to Friday, 9am to 8pm and Saturday, 11am to 5pm)

Maggie's Centres provide emotional, social and practical support and guidance to anyone affected by cancer through a network of local centres (which can be found through the map on the website). Local centres are the first and best point of contact. Some centres provide support to children through one-off days where they can meet other children living with a family health crisis.

www.maggiescentres.org

0300 123 1801 (Monday to Friday, 9am to 5pm)

Cancer Support – Scotland provides emotional and practical support on a one-to-one basis and through community-based groups to anyone affected by cancer including family, friends and carers; also direct support to anyone over the age of 16.

www.cancersupportscotland.org

0800 652 4531 (Monday to Friday, 9am to 5pm)

Tenovus Cancer Care / gofal canser provides practical and emotional support to people in Wales and other parts of the UK.

www.tenovuscancercare.org.uk

0808 808 1010 (Every day of the year, 8am to 8pm)

Cancer Focus Northern Ireland provides information to cancer patients and their families in Northern Ireland.

www.cancerfocusni.org

0800 783 3339 (Monday to Friday, 9am to 1pm)

SUPPORT FOR CHILDREN AND YOUNG PEOPLE WHEN SOMEONE IS SERIOUSLY ILL

Much of the support for children experiencing a family health crisis is available online. This includes:

www.riprap.org.uk is the website for Macmillan's support for teenagers when a parent has cancer. It carries information, stories of the experiences of other young people, has a directory of local sources of support and a moderated online forum for teenagers to talk to each other.

www.siblinks.org is an online resource for teenagers when a sibling (or a parent) has cancer. There is a moderated online forum.

www.themix.org.uk is a site crammed full of information and sources of support aimed at young people under 25 who are facing any challenge. It also offers support by phone, online or through social media. **0808 808 4994** (Every day of the year, 11am to 11pm).

www.hopesupport.org.uk is a youth-led charity aimed at supporting anyone aged 11 to 25 when a close family member is diagnosed with a life-threatening illness. The website shows what support is available in local areas.

FOR THOSE SUPPORTING CHILDREN AND YOUNG PEOPLE AFTER A DEATH

The Childhood Bereavement Network is the hub of all organisations offering support to bereaved children and young people. They have an online directory of local services.

www.childhoodbereavementnetwork.org.uk/directory

Winston's Wish offers guidance, information and support to those caring for a bereaved child through a Freephone National Helpline and a range of publications and resources (including memory boxes).

www.winstonswish.org

08088 020 021 (Monday to Friday, 9am to 5.30pm)

BOOKS AND RESOURCES

When someone is seriously ill

THE SECRET C: STRAIGHT TALKING ABOUT CANCER

By Julie Stokes OBE

This book is aimed at supporting parents or carers with trying to explain to their young children what cancer means and how it may affect their family.

WHEN SOMEONE HAS A VERY SERIOUS ILLNESS

By Marge Heegaard

A workbook to help children deal with feelings about serious illness. It is aimed at six to 10 year olds and is for use with a supportive adult.

FLAMINGO DREAM

By Jo Napoli

This book tells the story of a child's experience of their father's serious illness (including a final holiday together) until his death. For six to 10 year olds.

BENNY'S HAT

By Juliet Clare Bell and Dave Gray

This lovely, sensitive story about a sibling dying shows how siblings may feel and act when a brother or sister is seriously ill.

THE COPPER TREE

By Hilary Robinson and Mandy Stanley

This gentle, humorous story covers the serious illness and then the death of a primary school teacher and the way her school responds.

A MONSTER CALLS

By Patrick Ness

A powerful, moving and raw story for older readers about the feelings experienced by a boy as his mother is dying.

ONLY ONE OF ME – A LOVE LETTER FROM MUM / A LOVE LETTER FROM DAD

By Lisa Wells and Michelle Robinson. Illustrated by Tim Budgen/Catalina Echeverri

These beautiful and moving books (choose the appropriate one) are designed to support children by providing a comforting reminder of continuing love when a parent is expected to die.

THERE IS NO SUCH THING AS A DRAGON

By Jack Kent

A simple and effective story for younger children about the importance of talking about challenges facing a family before they become overwhelmingly large.

THE HUGE BAG OF WORRIES

By Virginia Ironside and Frank Rodgers

A story to encourage primary-aged children to talk about and share their worries.

'STEPPING STONES' POSTCARDS

Available from The Childhood Bereavement Network

These cards for young people offer suggestions and prompts on how to let others know how you are feeling when someone important is seriously ill.

Preparing to think about death

WHEN DINOSAURS DIE: A GUIDE TO UNDERSTANDING DEATH

By Laurie Krasny Brown and Mark Brown

This factual book, aimed at four to seven year olds, uses cartoon dinosaurs to explain death in a simple and non-threatening way.

NO MATTER WHAT

By Debi Gliori

A delightful story for three to eight year olds about a parent's unconditional love and reassurance that (in the original, older version) also gently introduces the idea of what happens to love after someone dies.